GETTING TO KNOW
THE WORLD'S
GREATEST COMPOSERS

THE
BEATLES

WRITTEN AND ILLUSTRATED BY MIKE VENEZIA

CHILDREN'S PRESS®
A DIVISION OF GROLIER PUBLISHING
NEW YORK   LONDON   HONG KONG   SYDNEY
DANBURY, CONNECTICUT

PHOTO CREDITS ©: AP/Wide World Photos: 6 bottom right, 6 bottom left, 24, 24 inset; Everett Collection: 3, 8 top right, 8 top left, 11, 14, 17, 19; Globe Photos: 30 (Frank Hermann/Camera Press), 32 (Bruce McBroom), 23 (NBC), 22 (Terence Spencer/Camera Press), 26; Hulton Deutsch Collection Limited: 10, 15, 31; Hulton Getty Picture Collection Limited: 21 (Steve Hale Photography), 4 (Bert Hardy); UPI/Corbis-Bettmann: 6 top right, 6 top left, 7 bottom, 7 top, 13.

Project Editor: Shari Joffe
Design: Steve Marton

Library of Congress Cataloging–in–Publication Data

Venezia, Mike.
    The Beatles / written and illustrated by Mike Venezia.
        p. cm. — (Getting to know the world's greatest composers)
    Summary: Tells the story of the world's most celebrated and
influential rock group.
    ISBN 0-516-20310-X (lib.bdg.)   0-516-26147-9 (pbk.)
    1. Beatles —Juvenile literature. 2. Rock musicians—England—
Biography—Juvenile literature. [1. Beatles. 2. Musicians.
3. Rock music.] I. Title. II. Series: Venezia, Mike.
Getting to know the world's greatest composers.
ML3930.B39V46   1997
782.42166`092`2—dc21
[B]
                            96-48492
                            CIP
                           AC MN

The Beatles, shown here on the album cover of *Sgt. Pepper's Lonely Hearts Club Band*, were probably the most celebrated rock group ever.

From about 1964 to 1970, the Beatles were the world's most popular musical group. The Beatles were four musicians from Liverpool, England. They were John Lennon, Paul McCartney, George Harrison, and Ringo Starr. None of them had any real music lessons. They pretty much taught themselves as they went along.

Liverpool in the 1940s

In the 1950s, when John, Paul, George, and Ringo were growing up, Liverpool was a poor, gloomy, seaport city. One good thing going on there was that local sailors returning home from their journeys brought back rock-and-roll records from the United States. People who lived in Liverpool became the first people in England to hear the exciting new music.

Rock and roll grew out of a bunch of different American musical styles, including country-western and African-American rhythm and blues. Rock and roll had a lot more energy, though, and a wilder sound. The favorite instruments of rock-and-roll groups were guitars, drums, and sometimes pianos and saxophones.

Long before the Beatles met, each of them was inspired by rock-and-roll music. They were crazy about singers like Buddy Holly, Bill Haley and the Comets, Little Richard, the Everly Brothers, Chuck Berry, Jerry Lee Lewis, and especially Elvis Presley.

Jerry Lee Lewis

Chuck Berry

Buddy Holly

Little Richard

Bill Haley and the Comets

It wasn't just the music itself that John, Paul, George and Ringo loved—the words of rock-and-roll songs made them feel good, too. Teenagers everywhere thought that rock singers understood them and had the same kinds of problems as they did.

Elvis Presley

John Lennon as a young child
(right) and with his mother (left)

John Lennon started the Beatles. He was born in 1940 during a World-War-II bombing raid. John's father left his family when John was only five years old. John's mother, Julia, felt her son would be better off being raised by his aunt and uncle.

John's mother stayed close to him while he was growing up, though. She helped him get his first guitar. Since Julia knew how to play the banjo, she was able to teach John to play his guitar a little.

John Lennon was known as a troublemaker in school. He was always getting into fights and arguments. John was smart, but he never got very good grades.

Later, John went to art college. He was a talented artist, but was really much more interested in playing his guitar and singing. John and his friends would practice their music in empty classrooms during lunchtime and after school. This was the beginning of John Lennon's band, which he called the Quarrymen.

The Quarrymen in 1955

A young Paul McCartney
(at left) with his mother and his brother Mike

Paul McCartney was two years younger than John Lennon. Even though music was always around Paul's home while he was growing up, he wasn't very interested in it until he became a teenager.

Paul's father led a small dance band and played the piano. He also rigged up a set of radio receivers for Paul and his younger brother. Paul heard his first rock-and-roll songs broadcast from far away as he lay in his bed late at night.

When Paul was fourteen, he started picking out his favorite tunes on the piano. He was pretty good at this, and soon was anxious to get a guitar. Once he got his guitar, it seemed like it was all he cared about. Paul practiced in any room he could find—even the bathroom!

One day, Paul heard a local band playing at a church picnic. The band happened to be the Quarrymen. Paul thought John Lennon was pretty cool. He noticed that when John forgot the words to a song, he would just make up his own words.

Later that day, Paul met John and played guitar for him. Paul imitated some famous rock-and-roll singers perfectly. John thought Paul was pretty cool, too, and asked him to join the Quarrymen.

Paul McCartney

George Harrison was the youngest Beatle. He was born in 1943. Of all the Beatles, George was the one whose parents were the most encouraging when he got his first guitar.

George started out by teaching himself to play. He often became discouraged, and almost gave up. Fortunately, his mother told him he would get it if he kept trying.

Six-year-old George Harrison (at right) with his older brother Pete

George Harrison at age twelve

By the time George was fourteen years old, he could play really well.

George happened to go to the same school as Paul McCartney. In fact, George's father drove the bus that took the boys there. George and Paul became good friends. They practiced their guitars at each other's houses. Paul introduced George to John Lennon. At first, John thought George was just a kid, and too young to pay any attention to.

But George had become good enough to get some jobs playing on his own. He kept hanging around the Quarrymen, hoping to become a member. One day, George played a rock-and-roll song that was one of John's favorites. John was so impressed that he said George could finally join the band. Now there were three members of the Quarrymen, who would soon become known as the Beatles.

The last member to join the Beatles was their drummer, Ringo Starr. Ringo's real name was Richard Starkey. He changed his name because he thought it sounded better for someone in show business. Plus, he always wore lots of rings!

Ringo had a pretty hard time growing up. He was born in 1940, and came from one of the roughest, toughest parts of Liverpool. When Ringo was six years old, he had a serious attack of appendicitis.

Ringo Starr as a child, with his mother

Then Ringo had some other illnesses that kept him in and out of the hospital until he was almost fifteen years old. He fell way behind in school, and had a very hard time catching up. Sometimes Ringo would play in the hospital band, but only when they let him play the drum. As a teenager, he became even more interested in playing the drums, and bought a set.

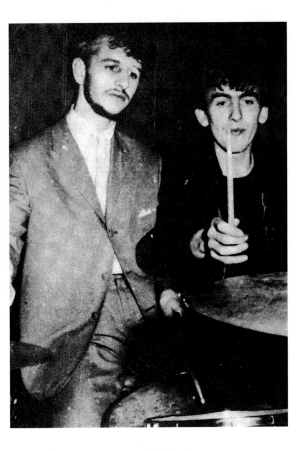

Ringo Starr and George Harrison before Ringo joined the Beatles

Ringo helped start a band that played mostly for the fun of it. Later he joined a band that became very popular in Liverpool. Ringo's new band would usually play in the same places as John Lennon's band, which was now called the Beatles.

The Beatles had a drummer, but John, Paul, and George weren't crazy about him. Sometimes when their drummer didn't show up, the Beatles would ask Ringo to sit in with them. John, Paul, and George got along great with Ringo and finally asked him to become their regular drummer.

Now the Beatles had everyone they needed to make a great rock-and-roll band. John played rhythm guitar. Paul played bass guitar. George played lead guitar, and Ringo played the drums.

Just before Ringo joined the Beatles, they had been having some luck playing in small clubs in Liverpool and in Hamburg, Germany.

These clubs were dark and dank, and sometimes were filled with creepy customers. The Beatles had to sing for hours at a time, late into the night. To keep themselves from getting worn out, the Beatles ate and drank right on the stage. They often told jokes to each other, and even yelled rude things at their audience! They were having a great time singing songs they had written and goofing around, and their fans loved it.

The Beatles (before Ringo joined them, with Pete Best on drums) on stage in 1961 at the Cavern, a small club in Liverpool

The Beatles, with manager Brian Epstein (top center),
after a long evening of performing

Suddenly, the Beatles were becoming a big hit around Liverpool. Now what they needed was a way to become better known outside of their hometown.

Luckily, a businessman named Brian Epstein came along at this time. Brian ran a record store down the street from where the Beatles were playing in Liverpool.

One day, he heard the Beatles, and thought they were great! Brian met with John, Paul,

George, and Ringo. He convinced them that he
could get their songs recorded by a big record
company. He also said he would set up concerts,
and would try to get the Beatles on radio and
TV shows. The only thing Brian asked of the
Beatles was to stop goofing around on stage so
much, and to dress
a little more neatly.
Brian Epstein
worked as hard as
he could to keep
his promise. Before
they knew it,
the Beatles were
playing their
music all over

England. They even played for the
Queen of England! Fans loved the way the
Beatles shook their floppy hair around and
sang their famous high-pitched "Ooooo."
Sometimes it caused some of their fans to faint!

The cheery "yeah, yeah, yeah" you can hear in their song "She Loves You" helped make it the Beatles first million-selling record. The Beatles were more popular than ever in England and the rest of Europe. There was one place, though, where the Beatles wanted to become better known.

Opposite page: Wherever they went, the Beatles were mobbed by screaming fans.

The Beatles on the "Ed Sullivan Show" in 1964

John, Paul, George, and Ringo really wanted their music to become popular in the United States—the country where rock and roll began. Brian went to work again. He talked to a famous television-show host in America, and arranged for the Beatles to appear on his show.

On the night the Beatles appeared on the "Ed Sullivan Show," it seemed like everyone in the United States was tuned in. The Beatles were a huge hit. The only problem was that fans in the audience were screaming so loud with excitement that people could hardly hear the Beatles sing. Now the Beatles were the most popular singing group ever! They began touring all over the world.

Traveling ended up becoming a big problem for the Beatles. Fans kept screaming so much that even the Beatles could hardly hear themselves sing. They always had to rush to and from their hotel rooms so they wouldn't get mobbed. Fans were everywhere! Also, traveling to so many cities all the time started making the Beatles cranky.

Finally, they decided to stop traveling and spend more time making records. This is when the Beatles' music started to change in an important way.

In the recording studio, the Beatles discovered and experimented with new sounds that had never been heard before. They used the recording studio kind of like an electronic instrument and created some of the most exciting music ever.

The Beatles tried things like putting echoes on their voices and recording their voices at different speeds. They experimented with the music of India and other cultures. They tried all kinds of different instruments, too. They brought in musicians from important symphony orchestras, and sometimes recorded things backwards. Their music had a huge influence on many rock composers who came after them.

In one of their greatest albums, *Sgt. Pepper's Lonely Hearts Club Band*, you can hear all kinds of wonderful sounds and lyrics the Beatles invented.

The Beatles, with producer George Martin, discuss work during a recording session in 1967. John and Paul composed most of the Beatles' songs, but George and Ringo wrote songs, too.

The Beatles performing the song "Hello Goodbye" in 1967

For the ending of a song called "*A Day in the Life*," the Beatles made a piano chord last for forty seconds. It sounds spectacular!

By the time the band broke up, in 1970, many people thought the Beatles had done something no other popular band had done. They had made popular rock-and-roll music as important as classical or symphonic music.

By the time the Beatles broke up in 1970, their superb melodies, catchy lyrics, and beautiful harmonies had earned them hundreds of hit songs. Their work had a huge influence on a wide range of rock groups that came after them.

In 1970, when the Beatles split up, it was just because they each wanted to try doing their own music. They were all very successful. Paul started a new group called Wings. George and Ringo recorded their own music and gave concerts. John wrote music with his wife, Yoko Ono. Sadly, John Lennon was killed by a deranged man in 1980.

Today, it's easier than ever to hear the Beatles' music. Their record albums have been re-recorded onto compact discs and tapes, and their music is on the radio all the time.